Dear Son, Dear Mom: Lessons I Learned from Somebody

Dear Son, Dear Mom: Lessons I Learned from Somebody

Uncomfortable Tales from a Son and His Mother Raising Each Other

Book 2

By Ron J. Fusselman and
Dr. Hilda Villaverde

Published by Pluma Designs
Scottsdale, AZ

Dear Son, Dear Mom: Lessons I Learned from Somebody
Uncomfortable Tales from a Son and a Mother Raising Each Other, Book 2

ISBN: 978-0-9669607-9-2 (paperback)

Library of Congress Control Number: 2020923472

Published by Pluma Designs
Scottsdale, AZ

LivingBrave.net
DearSonDearMom.com
hildavillaverde@gmail.com
rjfuss@gmail.com

Cover illustration by Grace Quest, graphic designer & illustrator, thegracequest@gmail.com

Book Shepherd Ann Videan, ANVidean.com

DEDICATION

We dedicate these words to Ron's grandmother,
my mother,
Maria Parra (Villaverde) Ramirez
October 13, 1924–August 19, 2018

In loving memory of her quiet strength, unconditional love for her children, pride and gratitude to live in the United States, and for her uncanny way of reigning over our family with one single sound:
Hummmmmm…

INTRODUCTION

HILDA

It is impossible to see what surrounds you when your eyes are closed. Honestly, little else in life opens your eyes wider than raising children.

As a youngster, I remember flinching and closing my eyes when sensing something coming my way that may hurt me. Perhaps my nose scrunched up and certainly my body tensed and pulled inward to guard myself. After all, it's a normal reaction to tense and pull away. No one likes pain, especially if they sense it coming.

For many growing up in tense and hurtful childhoods, their eyes remained closed even when they needed to be open.

As a young adult, I wondered why drama seemed to find me no matter how much I tried to escape its grasp. One painful event after another appeared to challenge my willing steps toward a healthy and happy life. Years later, I came to understand why I couldn't shake my "bad luck." My eyes were closed! Flinching and waiting for the something that would come to hurt me, I carried within me an internal belief, thoughts of impending danger coming my way. A pattern I formed as a child. No matter what steps I took, I anticipated the worst and, true to its formula, it came to me.

In our first book, *Dear Son, Dear Mom, Thoughts I Wanted You to Feel*, my son and I gave a microscopic account of our life together. We told our story and exposed our secrets of brokenness and struggles, and our subsequent recovery to a healthy and close relationship. It gave an overview of turbulent events that occurred to us even before his birth. As a child myself, only twenty-one when he was born, my eyes were certainly shut. I could not have perceived the immensity of my circumstances and the responsibility of giving birth to a child I was told to abort. With my eyes squeezed tight, body tensed and pulled inward—and in spite of the warnings I could sense—I became a mother.

We found our relationship as mother and son fraught with physical and emotional drama. The only way I knew to manage life was to dig in my heels and take the next steps forward. My desire to find the "Somebody" within myself—who would stand by me and lift me when I needed sustenance and comfort—pushed me headlong into the life my son and I created. Our journey drove us headlong into learning one lesson after another.

As my eyes began to open, a very slow process for me, I could see the "Somebody" we were both becoming.

In this, our second tiny book with a big message, we offer several detailed and uncomfortable tales that challenged us and ultimately brought us closer together. Raising each other, we flinched and stumbled and fell at the hits coming our way. Yet, we always came back to find that unexplainable calling for a mother and son to remain connected. No matter the country, culture, religion, or social, economic standing, mothers and their children pull apart during the growing process. Some remain disconnected, unable to mend the differences. Others take the demanding path of reconnecting. This disconnect is a natural progression of becoming the distinct person we are meant to be. An essential evolution for both child and parent in discovering their individual "Somebody."

In our first book, we also introduced Ron's "Somebody," a superhero character sketched as the expression of his thoughts and emotions. "Somebody" is also known by other names: inner voice, person in charge of thoughts, a tap on the shoulder, conscience, and so on. The truth is, we all want to be "Somebody," and we are all undeniably "Somebody." Outwardly, we express the signs of being the "Somebody" we want others to see by how we dress, what we drive, where we live, the work we do and, for some, the body art we wear. However, with all of the commonalities we share as humans—physical bodies, thoughts, emotions, senses, dreams, and desires—we are still distinctly the "Somebody" we choose.

Why did we write about our experience? Ron and I know the influence of stories. I grew up entrenched in the tales of my Mexican culture. Rich with drama, they always provided lessons for evolving into a better son or daughter, fighting the demons and witches that made us want to disobey our parents, and learning to obey and love our elders. I also heard the story of my parents and their struggles before immigrating to this country, and their adjustments after arriving. I cherish those tales now, knowing I am a creation of the genes, beliefs, and choices my parents made before and after my arrival in their lives.

When I began to read to Ron as a child, aside from telling him the stories of my childhood and of my parents, I read from *Miss Manners, Guide to Excruciatingly Correct Behavior*, a book written by Judith Martin in 1938. Since I had not been introduced to American fairy tales, I thought we could both learn something in this book of enquiries and responses. A client from the salon, who gave me the book, thought all children should be taught politeness and social graces.

Every night, we took on a question regarding etiquette and, at times, discussed it. We both learned. For years, Ron allowed me to read to him before he fell asleep. Perhaps the reading put him to sleep, or having his mother sitting next to him comforted him, as it did me. No matter. He listened and absorbed the quandaries presented to "Miss Manners," while I answered and compared any questions about growing up in my Mexican culture and about his grandparents. Our eyes opened wider and, together, we grew.

Ron developed a love for reading. He was never without a book from the time he could point to the words and enjoy the illustrations on the pages. What we both collected was an affection for people and their stories, and we felt a kinship beyond ourselves to others.

Stories connect us. Even the uncomfortable ones draw us to one another, perhaps even more so. They help us make sense of our frailties and give us common ground to stand together. They give us permission to make mistakes and fear less, knowing we are not alone. Stories soothe us and inspire us, they give us something to believe in. Mostly, stories open our eyes broader and help us see our surroundings from a different perspective.

Welcome to the second book in our series. We trust our uncomfortable tales will stir your thoughts and feelings, and open your eyes wider, as they have ours.

"Who sees all beings in his own Self and his own Self in all beings, loses all fear."
—The Isa Upanishad

CHAPTER ONE

LESSON 1: DUTY

Dear Son,

When you turned a year, your father and I bought a home in a not-so-good area of town. The criminal activity was high, the schools were challenged with gang rivalries, and the streets were unsafe. We realized this only after moving into the neighborhood.

The small red-brick house resided in a neighborhood of twenty new homes built by a speculating builder on a slight hill. We were the last homeowners to move into the community. The neighbors were all very nice and similar to us, most raising young children. Our small home consisted of a formal living room as you stepped into the front door, followed by a family room that opened to a galley kitchen to the left and three tiny bedrooms and a restroom down a hallway on the right. The master bedroom sat at the end of the hallway on the right with your bedroom situated on the left. A fence enclosed our small back yard away from the alley. A clothesline stretched across the back yard.

Your father traveled extensively, leaving you and me alone most of the time. One evening after dinner, when you were already in bed, your father talked about his concern for our safety while he traveled. We had heard of break-ins in our surrounding neighborhoods and he wanted to make sure of our protection. What I wanted was for him to be home with us and travel less. Instead, he unpacked a loaded gun from a case and explained how to use it in case of an emergency.

The gun would stay on top of the refrigerator where only an adult could reach. It would be ready to shoot if I needed it. He emphasized "emergency use only." He also gave me clear instructions.

"If you have to use this gun and you aim it, you must look as if you are serious and ready to shoot. Scream and yell, use every swear word you can think of while you muster up aggressive emotions, and don't take your eye off the person. Act as if you are out of your mind and insane with rage. Do not hesitate to use it if you or Ron are in danger in an emergency. When you fire, fire to protect yourselves!"

Five years earlier, at the age of eighteen while living in an apartment with a roommate, I'd experienced a break-in. We were two young women living in the city, attending school during the day and working evenings. One night at home all alone, a young man, high on drugs, came to my front door. Naively, I opened the door. He slammed it closed, grabbed me by the neck, and beat me for seventeen minutes. The neighbors—hearing my screams and wails of pain, my fists beating the walls and my feet kicking furniture—finally broke the door down and took him off me. I would never forget that event and, of course, feared being alone.

As your father explained the use of the gun to me, I dreaded such an event would ever befall me again. Even worse was the thought of having anything happen to you. But I decided then I would never touch the gun, no matter what. Even though it was during the time when Phoenix ranked close to or at the top of the list of cities with the highest crime rate. Kidnapping or human trafficking was not unusual because of our close proximity to the Mexican border.

A year later, on a Monday morning while your father traveled for the week, the dreaded event occurred.

I kept a routine of hand watering the plants in the front yard on Monday and Thursday mornings. Our desert landscaping did not have a sprinkling system, so I needed to hand water everything with a hose. You had been playing on your Big Wheel trike all weekend and it had collected dust and a bit of mud. You were very fond of the Big Wheel and I can still remember you peddling it down our driveway onto the sidewalk, and me chasing you down and around our block. At two years old, you brimmed with energy and loved being outdoors and active.

That particular morning, I put you in your bedroom down at the end of the hallway for your morning nap. I hurried outside to water plants and hose down the Big Wheel in front of the house.

Our home sat on a slight incline on the side of a hill. The street stretched just below at the end of our front yard beyond the sidewalk.

Busy watering, I looked up to notice a pickup truck with a camper shell slowly driving on our street. I did not recognize the man driving the truck through his rolled-down window. His hair fell long and scraggly almost covering his face, but I could see enough to make me uncomfortable. Three years prior, in 1971, Charles Manson had been convicted of first-degree murder and his "Manson Family" followers committed a series of nine murders at four locations. This man's face reminded me of his photos seen on television during the highly publicized trial.

As I stared at the camper on the back of the truck, I noticed a small window with a curtain and a woman's face looking out. Quickly she closed the curtain when she saw me staring.

The truck drove slowly until it made a right turn and disappeared. I was relieved.

A few minutes later the truck came by again. This time the driver nodded and smiled at me as they drove by. He gave me the creeps and I did not smile back. Again, I saw the woman's face at the camper window and again she closed the curtain. Instinctively, I looked to read the license plate, but it was missing.

This time the truck turned left at the end of the street. Relief flooded me again to see them go. I continued for another minute or so until it occurred to me the alley was behind our back yard on the left. They had turned left.

I dropped the hose and ran inside the front door. Immediately, I saw the truck driver standing at the back arcadia door leading to the back yard. His long hair hung over his face, he wore denim jeans and a long-sleeved washed-out blue shirt, and sported a tattoo on his neck.

He yelled at the woman headed down the hallway. "Get that f…ing kid!"

She wore a peasant skirt and a flowered blouse and sandals, popular then with the "hippie" generation.

I ran and grabbed the gun from atop the refrigerator and I did not need to pretend my mad rage!

Truth poured out of my mouth. I pointed the gun at the woman and yelled out with excruciating rage and fear, "You take one more f…ing step and I will blow your f…ing brains out!"

I screamed and yelled louder and he, still standing at the door motioning to her to keep moving and get the g… damned kid, screamed even louder. I could now see the knife hanging on his belt on his right side. Though scared to death, I was not stopping. There was no way I would allow them to take you from your bedroom.

I pulled back the hammer on the gun and, holding it with both hands, moved toward the woman. My yells came out even louder and with such insanity I could hardly believe what burst from my mouth. I swore I would shoot her right then if she didn't back the f…k down. I looked sideways to my left at the man in the door again. Feeling the rage intensify, I screamed I would also take him down like the disgusting man he was.

As I recall this incident and write these words, I cannot help but relive the fear and rage felt in that moment. Nothing can describe coming so close to losing a child and being willing to do *anything* to protect them, including killing someone.

She came toward me to move out of the hallway. I backed up a step but kept the gun pointed at her. I continued to scream and yell for them to get out of my f…ing home NOW!

He ran off first and she followed into the back yard through the baby clothes hanging from the clothesline. I followed as they jumped over the wooden fence and, still holding on to the gun, I made sure they got into the truck. As soon as they did, I heard you crying, wailing from your crib in the bedroom.

Exhausted with emotion, my heart racing, I ran down the hallway into your room. I grabbed you out of the crib where you stood, and pulled you out to hold you tight. We both cried.

We went back into the family room where I locked the doors and called the police. I placed the gun on top of the refrigerator once again.

Lesson One: Duty

I have thought of this incident repeatedly over the years. Each time I consider the question, could I have pulled the trigger? At what point would I have made that decision? I will never know. I do know that parenting is a serious responsibility.

The lesson I learned amounted to duty. I had a duty to protect my child, my "Somebody." I also have a duty to know when to let go and allow my child to become the responsible adult.

LESSON 1: DUTY

Dear Mom,
You're screaming very loud.
Fear and strength sounds in your voice.
Forty-four years later I will come to know that same fear and strength.
I will learn duty and what a parent will do to protect their child.
And I will be grateful to have been protected by you.

Chapter Two

Lesson 2: Keep Your Word

Dear Son,

This may appear to be a simple tale and only a snippet compared to the other stories, but the lesson has never lost its effective influence.

Keep your word.

I will begin this tale by saying a few words about disciplining a child. As a child growing up in a Mexican family with loving parents, challenged with scarcity, where emotions were reactive and drama was normal, my siblings and I were spanked. Spanked heavy-handed. When I became a mother, I believed in healthier ways of correcting and delivering consequences for a child's inappropriate behavior. I decided I would never hit my child improperly, but a swat on the bottom might be suitable to make a point. Now, as a grandmother with a better view of discipline—or better stated, correction and teaching—I find spanking unnecessary.

Even so, here is our uncomfortable tale about keeping your word.

You were a considerate child from the beginning, your personality sweet and cooperative. We founded our relationship on communication. You understood words and took direction at a very young age. We talked things out and discussed boundaries and rewards for being a good boy. Not that we didn't play hide and seek, tickle, play in the mud, read and draw, run, and sing loud in the car. We did, but my schedule in running our home, working, and taking care of my mother-in-law required us to stay on schedule as much as possible.

By age three you had learned to ask politely for what you wanted, saying please and thank you every time. Except at the grocery store one day, while sitting in the grocery cart, you started reaching for items without asking. It could have been boxed cereal, toys, cans, or anything bright and fascinating. This unusual behavior certainly wasn't working for me or for my schedule. It was so unlike you. I couldn't understand the defiance and felt myself blushing red at conducting a public argument with a three-year-old. Changes needed to be made soon.

Before our next grocery store run, we had a conversation. I assured you I knew you wanted items from the shelves, but grabbing for everything that caught your attention could not happen again at the grocery store, or any other store. Making a scene and arguing when you didn't get what you wanted was not going to happen anymore. It made me a nervous wreck, especially with my anxiety disorder. Besides, you had everything you needed at home, including food, toys, books, shiny things, etc.

I went over the consequences of what would occur if you acted out again while shopping. As soon as you started, the very first instant, I would park the grocery cart with whatever groceries we had, pull you out of the cart, and take you to the car. We would drive home and I would give you a spanking on the bottom. We would wait at home for you to stop crying and then return to the store to gather our groceries. This would happen. I asked if you understood this would make it hard for both of us. You nodded your head.

That little Somebody was only three years old, but I knew he understood.

As I write this, I can imagine psychologists criticizing me for the psychological damage I was imparting on your emotional well-being. In my defense, I did not have better skills and had yet to have any counseling of my own. I was naïve and desperate.

As expected, at the grocery store you began the inappropriate behavior, reaching and grabbing. Without any warning, I immediately parked the grocery cart with the checker in front of the store and let her know we would be back.

When you realized what was happening and I tried to pull you out of the cart, you screamed at the top of your lungs. "No, mommy. No, don't spank me! Please don't spank me!"

Holding on to the cart, I pried your hands open from the handle and walked out the door with you screaming. We made it to the car with people watching us. I'm sure, if cell phones had been invented, we would have gone viral and the police would have been called. With all the yelling and tossing your head about, I fully expected for somebody to come and grab you away from me.

We drove home with you in your car seat crying at a shrill pitch. It was terrible to hear you in so much pain but I had given you my word, there would be consequences for the behavior.

Arriving at home, you grabbed on to the car seat and I struggled to wrangle you out. The back seat of a Volkswagen Bug did not provide the easiest angle for maneuvering. I carried you into the house, still crying, set you down, and gave you a swat on the behind with my hand. Honestly, it hurt my heart more than it did your well-padded bottom. Plus, with my ears ringing from your shrill cry all the way home, I was hurting.

Trying to catch your breath in between your wails, I ordered you to your room until you could stop crying so we could go back to the store and gather our groceries.

Within five minutes, you came out of your room, sniffling and catching your breath, your chest bouncing up with every breath. You took my hand, looked up at my face and said you were sorry. You asked if we could go back to the store now. You were ready to behave.

Never again did you reach for anything from the grocery cart… ever. Not without asking. That was the only spanking you ever had. All I had to say was, "Don't make me take you home, Ron." Or I'd simply give you the "look" and somebody knew I would keep my word.

Later on, while you were in high school and six-feet tall, I tried to use the "don't make me spank you" tactic. You lifted me in your arms, threw me on the bed, and walked out of the room laughing. We both laughed at the absurdity of my comment. But the lesson had been learned and never forgotten.

Lesson Two: Keep Your Word

I learned people will stop hearing your warnings if they are empty words. Ron learned I meant what I said. The difference between saying you *will* do it and *doing* it are lessons well learned. As parents, we are the "Somebody" teaching right and wrong, safe and unsafe, appropriate and inappropriate. We must say what we'll do, then do it.

Lesson 2: Keep Your Word

Dear Mom,
Fear leads to growth.
I found this out at three years old.
Warned but forgotten, reminded again.
The evolution of a lesson I would learn with my own.

CHAPTER THREE

LESSON 3: FORGIVE IGNORANCE

Dear Son,

I wanted you to have the best education I could afford.

When you turned five, and your father and I divorced, I went from working part time to full time. I needed a place for you to stay after school while I worked. I placed you in private schools and, therefore, accomplished a better education and after-school care. Since you were sensitive and artistic, the smaller classrooms with more individual attention worked for you as well. It was a win for both of us.

I enrolled you, at age eleven, in a prominent Episcopalian private school where you entered the sixth grade. The school, well-regarded for its curriculum, offered exceptional teachers and exemplary Christian values. Although we did not attend a particular church, you were accepted as a student with the agreement you would attend daily church services with the rest of the students. You were not required to participate, but needed to sit in the back of the church during the service. Another sixth grader, a girl who was also not Episcopalian, sat with you in the back row.

You did very well with your studies and activities at the school your first year. Sixth grade was easy for you and your grades represented your commitment to doing well, and your ability to make friends and get along.

In seventh grade, something dramatically changed.

The school was located several miles from our home. I would drop you off at the school on my way to work, and either your stepfather or I would come by after school for pick up.

The first three months of school went along as things had the year before. You thrived in the classes and with your friends. In December, during Christmas vacation, you asked if you could change schools. When I asked if you were having a problem, you answered you just didn't want to go back. No reason, you just didn't want to.

I kept you in the school and, in January, just a couple of weeks after starting back, the principal called to ask me to pick you up early. In the office, you sat waiting. You had been dismissed for the rest of the week for fighting.

On our way home, I tried to talk about the incident. This had never happened before. You were not a boy who got into fights. Again, I pried for information. But you said nothing. You did not want to discuss it. You just didn't want to go back to the school.

As for the other student who had been in the fight, I called a friend who was a teacher at the school and was given some details. The boy was the same age and in the same classes, and much bigger, heavy and loud, and a bit of a bully. He was driven to school by a chauffeur and his family donated heavily to the church and school.

I insisted you go back to school, avoid this boy, and stop the fighting. A week later, the school called again, and you were permanently dismissed. When I tried to discuss the situation with the school principal, I met a brick wall. She had decided you needed to leave. There were no exceptions. Nor was there a conversation.

You remained silent on the way home and would not discuss it with me. I asked all the hard questions about this boy. Did he try to do something to you, did he call you names, did he touch you inappropriately? But nothing. You would not discuss it. Our evening reading routine stopped as well. You did not want me in your room. And there was no talking about it with you.

Your stepfather was upset with both of us, and angry the school terminated you. He felt personally embarrassed by the situation. There was criticism and yelling but still you would not talk. You simply shut down.

I scrambled to enroll you into a school, and moved you in with your father temporarily. He lived several miles from me, but close to a public school by his house where you would finish the year. You were not the same and our relationship began to disintegrate. You distanced yourself from me.

During this time, my husband and I bought a home in Scottsdale and moved. The upside involved a great public school for you just a mile from our new home. You could attend there, since you had made it very clear you would not attend another private school.

Because your father traveled, and you could not live with him permanently, you moved with us to Scottsdale. You insisted I not take you to school in Phoenix where you were still attending to finish the year. Instead, you took the city bus every day. I worried about you traveling for an hour every morning and evening, but you insisted and I conceded.

When the new school year started and you registered in the Scottsdale school by our new home, you insisted your father take you. You asked me to please not come by the school. You and your father would handle this. I obliged.

During this time—settling into our new home, school, and neighborhood; a new management position for me at a high-end hair salon; and problems in my marriage again—

you shared with me the reason for fighting at the Episcopalian school.

The bully had called you demeaning racial expletives. Worse yet, because the boy discovered I was Mexican, he loudly stated, "Your mother is a Spic and a stupid hairdresser. It doesn't take brains to be a hairdresser." He taunted you with these words and everyone in the school heard him. You defended yourself. Mostly you were defending me.

It devastated me to hear the cutting words. We sat with the feelings, and both broke down and cried. I could sense your relief of finally releasing the truth. You had carried the hurt of the accusation of being somebody less than others because of your mother's heritage.

Growing up in a small mining town in Arizona, my family had experienced the effects of discrimination, taunting, and segregation. But it had been years and my heart had forgiven and mended. Now this brought the feelings back for me. But my concern was for you. I could not imagine how you had kept this inside for so long. How much it must have hurt you, and still did, not wanting people to know our secret of being Mexican. You certainly didn't look Mexican, nor do I for that matter, but it felt as if there was something wrong with us. Unwelcomed.

Your father, a blond and blue-eyed German, served as the "Somebody" who connected you at your new school. I honored your wishes and not once did I attend any events or teachers' conferences. Of course it hurt, but you needed this time to heal your gaping wound.

As for me, I knew better. Only ignorant people mistreat others because of their race, color, or religious beliefs. My life experiences had given me examples of both prejudices and acceptance and I had forgiven the ignorant. Some day you would, too. It would take time to heal.

If I remember correctly, you were close to thirty when you discovered your love and appreciation for our Mexican heritage and the gift of being all of you.

Lesson Three: Forgive Ignorance

There will be hundreds of people who will interact with our children along their life path. We will not always be there to protect and advise them. Nor can we control the ignorance, beliefs, or behaviors of others. What we can do is offer our children a solid connection to us, to our own stories, and to the possibilities of becoming all they can be. We can be the "Somebody" who will be there for them as they learn to forgive themselves and others.

LESSON 3: FORGIVE IGNORANCE

Dear Mom,
Fights never resolve ignorance,
They only feed it.
Walk confident in your uniqueness, with no shame.
Educate with patience, knowing they might never understand.
Our differences help us navigate
What it is to be truly, individually, human.

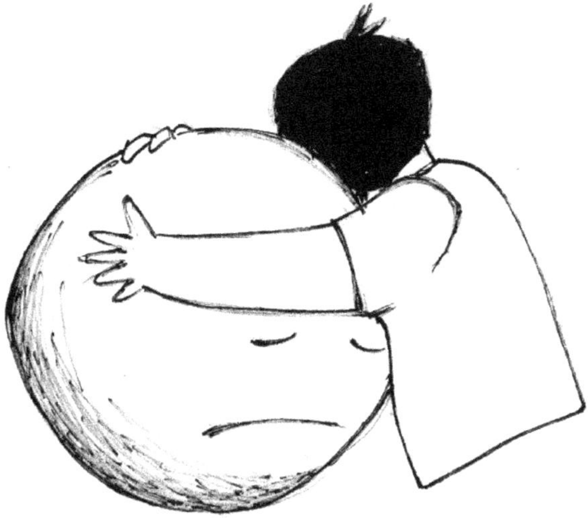

Chapter Four

Lesson 4: Bad Things Happen

Dear Son,

There is a saying that no one knows what goes on behind closed doors, except for those who live behind the closed doors.

By all appearances, when you and I moved in with my second husband, your stepfather, we believed it would be a better life for us. First, we lived in a beautiful new custom home in a very nice golf-course community. Second, he promised us financial security and the attention we both craved. Your father had traveled extensively and we had lived alone most of the time; we both craved affection, protection, and closeness. Here we found a man who would be home with us, and we could travel together as a family. I would work less hours and spend more time with you and our beautiful new home.

Within two years of our marriage, our life fell apart. Except for the beautiful home, the finances were short lived until the next "big deal" might come our way. The attention we received was manipulation to advance his career, and the travel also came with a price of advancing his standing in business—which was failing. I worked more hours to keep us afloat.

In our first book, you and I described the quick change in the temperament of my new husband. Demanding and hard to please, his bipolar disorder and addictions to alcohol, gambling, women—and eventually drugs—tossed our new family into a whirlwind of insecurity and anxiety.

In the eight-year marriage, glued together with promises, counseling sessions, gifts, travel, and more promises, you and I reached out to support his dreams. We stood by him as he reached countless successes, but mostly failures, in full view of our wide-open eyes. When he was good to us, he was protective and generous. His ambition, appetite for impressive living, and need for adventure carried us into experiences we could not have imagined. A private plane and a boat on the coast for our trips and the allure of expanding our previous small lives gave us hope.

Hope and despair took turns in a dance of trying to keep step with the music that played in his head. All the while, both of us sought approval and the attention and closeness we so needed. In his vulnerable times when failures came one after another, he needed us as well. He drew us in with tears and promises, and again we took up the dance and joined him.

I recall my thirtieth birthday morning. On that special morning, he brought me tea in bed with a beautifully wrapped box on a tray. He professed his commitment to me, to both of us, as a husband and father to you. I believed him. Inside the box, I found a stunning diamond ring worth more than my car. Though I suspected he was seeing other women, he always insisted he wasn't. I wanted to believe him, so I decided to believe him for that day.

He was extravagant and his ego required him to show off a wife wearing a large diamond ring and driving a Mercedes Benz. But inside of him lived a lost child, who came from an alcoholic family. Ignored and lacking attention and direction, he too craved being loved and accepted and being "Somebody."

The tight reins he held on you were his way of controlling, not just you, but his own fragile destiny. Always a day away from his mania or depression, the cycles of uncertainty and disaster weighed heavy on him and on us.

I know you looked up to him when he was at his best. Your sensitive nature reached out to him and, over and over again, you became vulnerable to his chastising verbal abuse. Overlooking it to find the respect you held for him, you flinched and closed your eyes and waited. Your good manners and social politeness gave him an edge when entertaining and networking clients for his search and recruiting firm. You served him well by entertaining his clients' children on the boat in San Diego and you were the son he always wanted, but never had.

His charismatic and uncanny ability to get what he wanted, made him the man to watch and admire. The times he encouraged you were few and far between, and I know you valued those words when he did. He was not a monster. He was bright, with an amazing shrewd and creative mind, until he plunged into his darkness. And then his monsters took over and we all suffered.

I do believe you and I gave it our very best. We tried to stay with him and weather his dangerous storms. But his addictions got the best of him and we left broken from being tossed around within the tornado of emotions he embodied. We were broken to pieces when we left. He disappeared completely leaving us in financial and emotional ruin, mainly because we loved him.

Gathering ourselves and starting over again, you and I would ultimately find our way and came to believe in ourselves again. We would become our "Somebody" and give our love again.

But we would never forget the "Somebody" he had been in our lives.

Lesson Four: Bad Things Happen

When you live long enough and can understand life from different perspectives, you come to know that every life story includes bad things. These trials happen for parents and their children equally. Do bad things happen to you or for you? Your interpretation of this question will rule how you live and how you will treat others. This will become your story and the "Somebody" you turn out to be.

LESSON 4: BAD THINGS HAPPEN

Dear Mom,
Opulence disguised anger, torn down, never to be brought back up,
Searching for things never to be found.
Left empty and drained,
The repercussions lasting decades.
Finally, like a Phoenix finding love, resurrected in the fire,
Life lessons I've discovered.

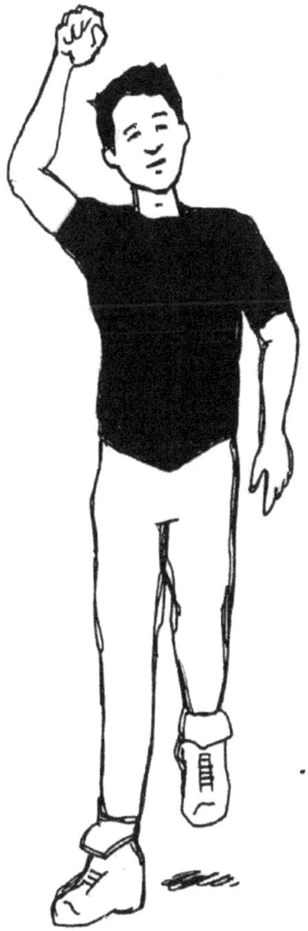

Chapter Five

Lesson 5: Pray

Dear Son,

I did not want you to play football. I felt it was too dangerous. I had read the data on head injuries and concussions. On and on I went defending my stance, insisting you not play the sport. Your father had played high school football in his small town in Pennsylvania and was awarded a scholarship to the University of Southern California where he played for three years until injured. He also hoped to become a walk-on player with the Dallas Cowboys. He did not make the team, but came close. Football was his game. Still, I insisted you would not play. I would not sign the papers the school required.

You began playing soccer at the age of seven. It was a great sport for you and one I could accept. I believed it was safer for your body and brain. You learned the intricacies of team sports including losing well and winning with consideration for others. Both your father and stepfather enjoyed attending the games and watching you flourish on the field. Outside of soccer, you enjoyed golf, basketball, tennis, and racquetball. You are a natural athlete.

When entering high school, you once again asked if I would change my mind and allow you to add football to your school sports. I said no. Three years later, your father signed the papers for you to join the varsity football team in your last year of high school. As soon as I heard the news, I began to pray you would not play one minute of the sport. There was nothing else I could do.

I came into this world knowing how to pray. My mother prayed continuously. In the true Mexican culture, few conversations did not include the mention of God, *Dios*. The answer to every question included, *"Con el favor de Dios,"* with God's favor.

"How are you?"

"Well, *con el favor de Dios."*

"How are the children?"

"They are all well, *con el favor de Dios."*

"Where are you going on vacation this summer?"

"La Jolla, *con el favor de Dios."*

Reference to God was a natural and automatic connection to Him, to hope, a belief, reliance, and at times an appeal. God's favor permeated our lives, He was the only reason we lived.

I found it interesting that this interchange and reference to God did not translate to the English language as easily and as automatically for me. I never heard myself say the words "with God's favor" after a question, unless I was speaking Spanish. Even so, I knew about prayer.

Years later, I studied spiritualty and a diversity of religions as I followed a course of study through Emmerson Institute for a doctorate in religious studies. An interesting principle discovered in the New Thought religion involves every thought we have serving as a prayer of sorts. Whether we curse a situation or we hold it up to a greater outcome, our thoughts form a sort of petition, belief, reliance, or outcome.

You began football practice in the intense heat of the Arizona sun, weeks before the football season started in September. Two practices a day, morning and evening, the team worked relentlessly to be in the best shape ever. Your appetite increased and shopping costs at Costco doubled to provide enough food to keep you fed. Your life revolved around playing football. You were determined to prove you deserved to play with a team that had already played together. You did it. As you told me at the time, it was the best shape you had ever been in. You were ready to play. I kept praying.

Friday, a week before the first game, I was preparing for a weekend in San Diego. A couple had asked me to join them at their rental house on the beach for Friday and Saturday. Your father would come by the house for you that evening after football practice, and you would spend the weekend with him. It was all set.

Just before practice that afternoon, while home packing for my trip, I heard the garage door open and knew you were home. Coming into my bedroom, you asked me for your weekly allowance.

I shook my head. "You will not be getting an allowance this week. As you can see from the list on the refrigerator door, you have not accomplished your chores for this week and money has been deducted."

Of course, you were angry.

Towering over me, you yelled, "I can't believe you would do this to me. It's the weekend before the first game and you're leaving town. What are you thinking?"

I reminded you I was thinking we had an agreement. You did not do your chores. You did not take care of the dog, clean up after yourself, or make your bed. You knew what was expected. The list stayed on the refrigerator door for you to see, every day the same was expected.

You rolled your eyes and walked out of my bedroom and out the garage door, still yelling, and drove off in your car.

I prayed you would be safe.

Five minutes later, you came back. I was still in the room packing. You walked in and said you wanted me to reconsider giving you some money.

I kept my word and said I would not. "This was not my doing, but yours, and you had a responsibility to us as a family."

"I hate you!" you spat as you walked out the door once again.

As I heard you drive off. I prayed again you would be safe.

That evening at the airport I couldn't stop thinking of our conversation. It was painful to hear the words "I hate you." Of course, you were angry and you didn't mean it, but it hurt. We were trying to recover our relationship and I had set us back. Should I have given you money and not held you to your word? I caught my train of thought and went back to praying, and thinking of all the good about you, about us. I reminded myself I was a good mother. Though strict, I was doing what I knew was the best I could. I was teaching accountability. Somebody had done that for me at a very young age. Most likely my mother.

As my plane took off a few minutes before nine that evening, a strong heaviness weighed in my chest. I found it hard to breath. I thought it might be the rapid climbing of the airplane or a bit of anxiety about leaving you in such a state of anger. It took me a while to recover my normal breathing and I thought to call you at your father's home when I arrived in San Diego.

My friends picked me up at the airport and we went out for dinner. By the time we came to their home it was late and I had forgotten to make the call. This was before cell phones.

At six in the morning, the phone rang in the house. I didn't think much about it. After all, it wasn't my home.

The husband knocked at my door and said it was your father. My heart pounding, I answered the call.

"Is he okay?" came out as my first comment.

He answered yes, though there had been a car accident. You were fine and you wanted to talk with me.

You came on the line and said you were so sorry while gasps of sobbing interrupted your words. As the car was hit and rolling down a ditch, throwing you into the windshield, you thought of the words you said to me. You didn't want to die and leave those as the last words I had heard. Because they weren't true. You wanted me to know how much you loved me. We stayed quiet for a moment as we both let the words sink in and I knew how much we loved each other.

Just before nine, on the way home from football practice, you drove brothers Jeff and Jeremy home. No one wore seatbelts. On a busy street, you came up to a green light and began to cross when a large truck turned left in front of your Honda Civic and hit you. The impact tossed the car and rolled it into a large expansive ditch. The force propelled your face into the windshield, cutting your forehead and creating cuts and bruises on your upper body. Your foot caught in the brake pedal, twisted, and broke the bones in your ankle.

Jeremy and Jeff were unhurt, but you could not move. Jeff ran to my home where your father waited for you. An ambulance took you to the hospital and paramedics wrapped temporary bandages on your ankle to hold your foot in place. They let you go home several hours later, knowing you would need surgery.

Two weeks later, surgery included two pins to hold the ankle in place. Although you attended the football practices and sat on the sidelines for the entire season, you did not play one minute of the sport.

Months later, when the doctor released you to participate in sports once again, you played with your varsity soccer team. The team ranked number one in the state. To this day, you have the pins in your ankle.

Lesson Five: Pray

As parents, we will experience the pleasures as well as the frustrations of raising our children. We will need anchors. My personal anchor is prayer: my conversation and connection for the highest and best outcome for all involved. Every trial and tribulation has led me down my path to looking inward and relying on the God I have come to trust. *"Con el favor de Dios."*

LESSON 5: PRAY

Dear Mom,
An unknow prayer,
A perception of failure,
Turns into a flower,
Far from the truth.
The power of thought
Exists in eternity,
Constantly creating
Our every move.

Chapter Six

Lesson 6: Attention to Details

Dear Son,

Although we were still struggling to connect with each other during our post-divorce trauma, high school became a welcomed playground for you. You had lots of friends to hang out with, as well as sports, trips, and dating. Popular, even with the parents of your friends, they invited you to travel with them and spend time at their homes. They enjoyed having you around, and said you were a good influence on their children, always well-mannered and polite. The years reading Miss Manners surely contributed. You became very independent and your confidence began to grow.

With our relationship on shaky ground after our time in my second marriage, I could sense you didn't trust me to make good decisions for us. I also understood your journey transforming from a boy into a man at the time. Hormones raging, a sense of your creativity emerging, and new friendships for both of us stirred our emotions and separated our lives more than I liked.

In our home, I needed to establish myself as the parent and lead person. It was a crucial time for a single mother and her son to continually establish the margins of love and discipline. We disagreed daily on something, mostly your new independence and the way we would manage living together in our small home. I firmly worked to hold the position as your mother, a strong mother with expectations, rules, and boundaries—trying to direct you safely during this time of growing up. At the same time, my own stability after a second divorce required my own adjustment.

One way for me to lead as your parent was to establish how, together, we would manage our home. We both had chores to accomplish. You took care of our dog, Max, cooked your meals, and cleaned up after yourself in the kitchen, and kept your room organized. I worked more than full time, and took care of the rest of the house with help from our housekeeper. I made sure we had what we needed to live comfortably, although it wasn't enough compared to your new friends' lifestyles. I stood out as the only divorced parent in your group of friends.

One of our morning rituals included arguing about making your bed before leaving for school. Your defense, that you would be back in the bed that evening, was a strong one, but I was firm in enforcing your responsibilities. Accomplishing your chores determined your weekly allowance. I posted the schedule for chores on the refrigerator door and there were few exceptions. You started off with an amount in your weekly allowance account and if a chore was not completed, I subtracted money. Occasionally, I let some things slide but, for the most part, we stayed the course of working together to keep the house organized, care for the dog, and provide a nice home. I truly needed and appreciated your help around the house.

Making your bed had become our signature disagreement.

"After all," I argued, "making the bed is about learning the value of ownership, and it's a sign of gratitude. It's also how you build self-discipline. 'How you do one thing, you do everything,'" I said to you. "You're fortunate to have a bed to sleep in every night. Millions of children in the world can only wish for such a luxury. Why not express your appreciation for the simple possessions in life, like a comfortable and well-made bed?"

I never did need to present the "eat all your food on your plate, there are people starving in China" argument. You always ate everything on your plate.

"Self-discipline is what separates achievers from non-achievers," I told him. "Achievers do the tough things nonachievers choose not to do, and that can be as simple as making a bed."

It was the best argument I had. Sometimes I won and sometimes you won. When you left the bed unmade, I would deduct money from your allowance. It was our agreement.

A month after high school graduation you moved to San Diego to attend a junior college. Gone for two years making some good and some not-so-good choices and working through them, you became even more independent and self-confident. But you were unsure of what career to follow. You came back to Arizona and roomed with a few friends while you attended Arizona State University. You studied three more years and worked in restaurants as a server and bartender.

I could see your struggle with school and a career choice but waited for you to make a decision. One morning you called to say you were coming by to talk to me about something you were considering. You had been taking some art classes, but mostly business courses. I had encouraged you to study business, suggesting that knowing how to run a business wouldn't hurt no matter what career you followed.

During this time, an important component in our relationship involved you coming to me for advice. At least I felt included in your decision making. I had longed for this connection since our relationship had begun to unravel during my divorce from your father and my second marriage and subsequent divorce. Healing had been a long time coming.

So, we sat and talked and made a plan for your future.

At the age of twenty-four you applied and were accepted to the prestigious Art Center College of Design in Pasadena, California, a well-respected, internationally acclaimed college. Admittance did not come easily, as it required letters from your high school—in particular your art teacher, who had been a thorn in your side. But, that is for another story. Art Center was an expensive education and, with a bit of help from me, you settled into Pasadena and began a four-and-a-half-year immersion in design and the art industry.

Most of the students attending the Art Center were your age. Many, as you, had attended other colleges and now knew they wanted to be in the arts. The school imposed a high expectation from students. Those attending were asked not to work outside of their school studies. The rigorous classes demanded added attention to projects produced on a regular basis. Most of the attendees came from Asia, Japan, and Taiwan, and other countries outside of the United States. Most had plenty of money and did not work. I recall our conversations about the high-end cars such as BMWs and Mercedes parked in the school parking lot. You worked the entire time and drove a Honda Civic. My heart overflowed with pride for you.

You rented a small "garage" studio, in the back yard of a bohemian Mexican Indian woman's home. When I met her on one of my visits, she reminded me of me, as she also came from a Yaqui Indian tribe in Mexico. No matter, the studio smelled of natural gas, and we never could figure out from where the smell came. You were settled, working, and attending your dream school.

During your first months at the Art Center, you commented on one of the professors, Mr. Osaki, a very successful businessman from Japan. He demanded much from his students and pushed them hard to pay attention to the details. All of the students respected his keen eye for design, welcomed his direction, and appreciated any appraisal of their work. All were eager to please him.

Several months later, you voiced a concern about your class with Mr. Osaki. "I see him stopping at other students' work stations, making comments and giving advice, but he doesn't stop at mine. I don't know what is going on."

I asked you to consider meeting with Mr. Osaki to let him know you needed his attention. You said you would think about it, but felt hesitant. No one questioned this professor, and you didn't want to start off on the wrong foot or appear insecure or, worse, incapable.

I encouraged you to make the time with him and ask. After all, you were there to learn and you wanted all the education and feedback you could get, especially from someone you respected so highly. If you don't ask, you don't get. Not to mention the amount of money you paid to attend.

A couple of weeks later, you talked with Mr. Osaki and asked why he had been ignoring your work.

He answered with a question, "Do you make your bed?"

You answered, "Why do you ask?"

"I can tell," Mr. Osaki answered and walked away to the next student.

In sharing the conversation with me, you asked for my advice. I suggested you begin making your bed each and every morning, and consider what that might mean to Mr. Osaki. Two months later, you reported Mr. Osaki had begun stopping by your workstation to make comments and give direction. I never asked if you were making your bed.

Four years later on graduation day, I had the opportunity to meet Mr. Osaki. I could feel the intensity of his standards and the pride he held for the students. I thanked him for taking the time with you. He was another "Somebody" you would never forget.

Lesson Six: Attention to Details

It's been more than twenty years since that graduation day. Since then, Ron has enjoyed a rewarding career in the film industry in which discipline and attention to detail have been important factors to his success. That wise saying, "How you do one thing, you do everything," still resounds. Thank goodness my "Somebody" taught me to pay attention to details as I grew up. Thanks to my mother.

LESSON 6: ATTENTION TO DETAILS

Dear Mom,
Decisions made,
Trust is lost and then found.
Directions are given and then ignored.
The love between a mother and son moves things forward.
Time passes over us like water, buoyant yet influential.
Valuable lessons taught for a second time,
Their value finally revealed.
You saw the future before I did.

CONCLUSION

LESSONS FROM SOMEBODY

Dear Son,

We began writing our first book; *Dear Son, Dear Mom, Thoughts I Wanted you to Feel*, in the beginning of the COVID 19 pandemic. Both of us stayed in our homes in seclusion, with you and Yvonne in California with a sixteen-month-old son and a baby girl due in six weeks. You were all hunkered down for however long it would take for safety to return.

I stayed in my home in Arizona for five weeks, away from my salon business. When I returned to work, it was slow going. Most clients were afraid to schedule appointments. We worked only a few hours a day, and felt grateful to be working.

You and I discussed telling our tale and writing a small book during this time, and we both thought we would enjoy working together again. Writing would give us a slice of relating, aside from the social distancing and implausible fear looming over us. Not that you didn't have your hands full already with the new baby "Somebody" and a new "Somebody" on the way. But we agreed to give a book some time and attention. We mused and agreed collaborating might also stir our creative juices aside from our current occupations. We did not expect to unearth the memories and emotions we thought we had left behind long ago.

Recalling the events leading us to raise each other, we discussed feelings while reviewing the circumstances of our painful times. This included the break-in when you were two, which of course you did not remember. But I never forgot my "duty" to protect you. Nor did you recall the grocery store lesson of "keeping your word." You simply knew I kept my word.

I must confess I struggle with "forgiving ignorance." Especially when I think someone is perceiving me as the ignorant one. I can only hope they forgive me. After all, this is what I know as my reality at this time, and so it is the same for everyone else. We each manufacture our reality from all of the days we've lived thus far. One thing I know for sure, time changes our views and relaxes our opinions… or not. Nonetheless, I want forgiveness for my transgressions due to my own ignorance, as much as I want to forgive others.

I'm far from being a perfect mother. As a matter of fact, after writing and publishing our first book and digging up our murky past for all to read and form an opinion about our lives and my motherly acumen, I was surprised and relieved by the comments of mutual association. Most mothers could relate to digging in their heels, making dangerous decisions, divorcing, or simply trying to control the consequences that may befall their children. After all, as mothers, we have dreams and desires, and the need for safety and control of our surroundings and for our children. Bad things happen to everyone. And good things come, even from bad things.

I have no personal need for anyone to have faith in God. I know I rely greatly on my belief in God, and in prayer. It gives me a sense of connection, communion, and reliance on that which created the universe—and every tiny and vast thing in it, including me and every single person who has landed in my heart and thoughts for my entire life. More times than not, my faith has made me so happy I could explode with joy. That is when I pray in gratitude for the life I have been given.

Other times, I pray with deep sadness for what I think would be a better outcome. I recall pleading with God to take our mother to heaven sooner than later. My siblings and I prayed for three years for this outcome without a response.

The day our mother passed was the perfect day. I had been with her just a few hours earlier and laid in bed with her, held her, and let her know how precious she was to all of us. I told her we loved her unconditionally and we would see each other again. I was sure of it. Our prayers were answered the next morning. The timing was flawless.

Some call prayer meditation. Others know it as self-talk, positive thinking, communication with the higher self or the wise counselor, or an invocation or a petition seeking to activate a bond with the entity that hears our voice. I have come to know every thought is a form of deliberate incantation, a prayer of sorts, and a personal relationship with the part of us who knows our finest selves. When I pray, I talk to the God I have come to know, and I reconnect with the source of me that knows what is best for all involved. I prepare for the highest outcome.

As a new parent, you now understand the lessons that come with the responsibility of having children. Eyes wide open, as a father you will sense the duty to protect, keep your word to them, forgive their innocent ignorance, embrace them when bad things happen and you will pray. I know you will.

Attention to details can be a thorny lesson. For some, it is the natural rhythm of being themselves. Eyes open to surroundings and a view of the world both complicated and worth examining, these individuals are born paying attention. But there is a price to pay. No one is perfect, and attention to the details and a desire for the perfect outcome—both from oneself and others—can be a prickly and bumpy journey. We all have our lessons to discover.

Then there are those of us forced to pay attention to the details. In the introduction, I stated I grew up with my eyes tightly closed, flinching for the next thing to come my way that might hurt me. Nowadays, I no longer wait for that thing to come my way. I am secure in the fact that bad things happen and, most likely, something will come that will tug at my heart and fill my mind with unease. At that time I will open my eyes wider and see beyond the problem to discover another lesson from "Somebody." One of many lessons worth mentioning here on paying attention is knowing when to hold on and when to let go.

Paying attention to each other has been the life line of our essential human existence. We need to connect and bond with one another to keep our world recreating. We are meant to share our joys and our concerns, our successes, and failures, and we need to share our stories. After all, we all need "Somebody" to love and love us back. In the end, our life journey is all about relationships. More than physical health or the environmental impact on our lives, the greatest influence to living a healthy and extended life are close relationships and social interactions. We grow and thrive through our hours of relating, on our way to becoming our own "Somebody."

It has been my pleasure working on a second book with you, Ron. Not every mother has this privilege, and I do consider it a privilege to have this bond with you. During my many years, I've heard stories from women whose sons are no longer available to them through tough consequences. Heart wrenching tales of loss have come my way, deepening my gratitude for what I have with you and your beautiful family.

I am grateful for your open heart in sharing your words, and not hesitating to expose our lives for others to feel our uncomfortable tales as we raised each other. After all, we are all in this together, learning how to live as "Somebody."

Love you,
Your Mom

Lessons from Somebody

Dear Mom,
It has taken a lifetime for it to make sense to me,
Our pain, tears, love, and overwhelming joy.
Our journey together has never been boring,
Through it all, we held each other tight,
And we have pushed each other away.
Lessons learned, a bond forged in iron,
I wouldn't change a thing
As long as it is your support I am left with.

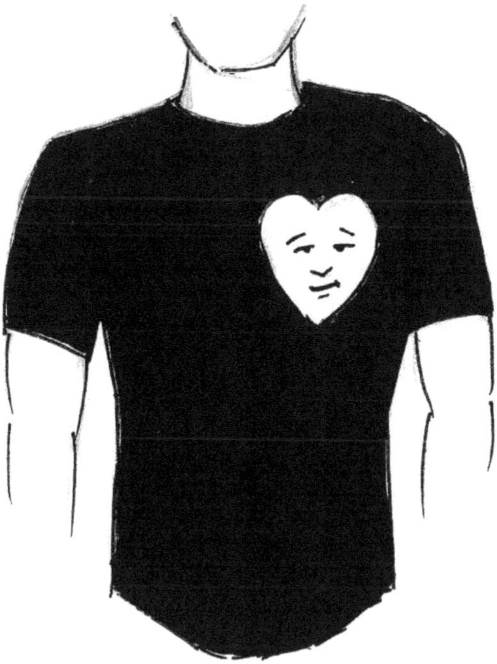

Request for Reviews

If you enjoyed this book, please consider jotting a review on Dr. Hilda Villaverde's book page at Amazon.com.
Even a couple of sentences about your experience will be most appreciated.

Also, feel free to contact us through our website at DearSonDearMom.com.

About the Authors

Dr. Hilda Villaverde is the author of nine published books. She earned her doctorate in religious studies with a minor in pastoral counseling at age fifty-five. Blessed with the gift of gab, Hilda is a recognized public speaker and captivating storyteller. Maintaining a successful business in the beauty industry for more than fifty years, she continues to stand behind the chair doing what she loves... hairdressing. True to her Mexican heritage and its reverence for family, Hilda also absolutely loves being a grandmother and the best mother-in-law she can be.

Ron J. Fusselman lives in San Diego, California, and for more than twenty years has worked in the design and film industries, producing and assisting in the creation of a variety of artistic endeavors in Hollywood. He also directs and produces his own content for film and television. Ron earned his bachelor of fine arts degree from the Art Center College of Design in Pasadena, California. His love of art first materialized at the age of two on restaurant place mats, and even the walls at home became his canvases. He and his beautiful wife, Yvonne, have a son and a daughter.